AF752853

About this Book

This is the story of the history and way of life of a rare kind of whitetail deer living on a group of sea islands off the coast of Florida. They are the smallest deer in North America, only about the size of a large dog.

How did these deer become so small? Read about what might have happened to change the size of the deer living on the islands thousands of years ago and how the tiny deer were recently saved from extinction by thoughtful people who cared about them.

The illustrations of this book show you the Key deer living in their natural habitat today.

ISLANDS of the TINY DEER

JULIAN MAY

Illustrated by Rod Ruth

YOUNG SCOTT BOOKS

Text Copyright © 1972 by Julian May. Illustrations Copyright © 1972 by Rod Ruth.
All Rights Reserved.
Young Scott Books, Addison-Wesley Publishing Company, Inc., Reading, Massachusetts 01867.
Library of Congress Card Catalog No. 71–179368. ISBN: 0–201–09233–6.
Printed in the United States of America.
Second Printing.
GO/BP 09233 12/73

THIS BOOK IS FOR *H.A.S.*, TOO.

For tens of thousands of years, North America has been the home of the whitetail deer. They are beautiful animals, with coats of grayish- or reddish-brown. When they are surprised, they raise their tails. The underside of the tail is brilliant white and flashes a warning to other deer nearby, as if to say: "Be alert! Danger may be near."

Whitetail deer are among the most abundant large wild animals in North America. They live from middle Canada to Panama, from the Atlantic Coast to the edge of the Great Basin deserts of the West. They are least common in the drier parts of the western states; Alaska has very few.

Full-grown Whitetail Deer

BUCK: *weighs 175–200 pounds and stands about 38 inches high.*

DOE: *weighs about 125–160 pounds and stands about 34 inches high.*

Full-grown Key Deer

BUCK: *weighs 70–100 pounds and stands about 30 inches high.*

DOE: *weighs less than 70 pounds and stands about 28 inches high.*

One kind of whitetail is quite rare and different from all the rest. Down south of Florida, on sea islands called the Florida Keys, live tiny whitetail deer weighing about half as much as their northern relatives. Key deer are the smallest of their kind, only about the size of large dogs. Their coats are brown, with white on the underside of the body and tail and dark markings on the face. They have large, gentle eyes that see well in the dark and sensitive ears that listen carefully to the sounds about them.

The islands of the tiny deer have warm weather all year round. Many kinds of palm trees and other tropical trees and plants grow there. The deer share their islands with only a few other wild mammals. On land, there are pale-furred, crab-eating raccoons, water rats, mice, and shrews. The waters between the islands have groups of warm-blooded, playful porpoises. Flocks of birds are everywhere; butterflies flutter among wild flowers during all months of the year.

Instead of having four seasons like most of the rest of North America, the islands have only a dry season and a rainy season. From December to April, very little rain falls. Then storms begin to build up over the tropical ocean and sweep northwest to the Keys. Most of the showers are brief, but they dump a great deal of rain on the islands.

The rain is the water of life to the Key deer. Their islands have no rivers. Rainwater, caught in rocky pockets in the ground, is all they have to drink.

Just before the rainy season begins in May each year, many of the young of the Key deer are born. The female, called a doe, finds a quiet place among the shrubs. One, or more often two, fawns are born. They are only about the size of house cats, but their legs are very much longer.

The doe licks her newborn young. The babies are bright reddish-brown, with white spots on their backs. Their eyes and ears are open and they can stand and walk a little soon after birth. The mother deer has an udder, something like that of a cow, with four nipples. The fawns suck milk from the nipples, wagging their little tails eagerly. When they are full, they settle down on the ground and go to sleep. Their mother walks quietly away to feed.

For the first few days after birth, the fawns are too weak to follow her. She leaves them resting among the tropical shrubs, their spotted coats blending with the pattern of light and shade. There are no animal enemies to bother them.

Several times each day she visits them to let them nurse. During the daytime, she herself rests a short distance away. At night, she goes off to eat.

Like all whitetails, she is a browsing animal, feeding on leaves and the small twigs of trees and shrubs. The favorite Key deer food is red mangrove, a tree that grows in shallow salt water at the edges of the islands. She eats other plants as well, and also the fruits of wild shrubs.

Stepping easily through the warm darkness, the doe can find all of the food she wants within an hour or so. Finding fresh water is not so easy. It has not rained in several weeks. Most of the shallow waterholes in the island rocks have gone dry. The doe must walk more than a mile to a larger watering place, a pond hidden among large gumbo-limbo and strangler-fig trees.

Other Key deer are there, drinking. At this time of year, many of the Key deer bucks have begun to drop their antlers. Two flat, red spots on top of their heads mark the places where the antlers have fallen away. Among all whitetail deer, only the males have antlers. And these are shed each year, then grown again.

When the mother doe has drunk her fill, she goes back to the place where she has left her twin fawns. She lets the little ones nurse, then lies down some distance away to chew her cud. Earlier, she had swallowed her plant-food very quickly, without chewing it much. The food was stored in a special stomach until she had time to finish her meal. Now, as she rests, she brings the food up again a mouthful at a time and chews it well. When the food is swallowed this time, it passes into three other stomachs and is digested.

Northern whitetail deer sometimes have difficulty finding enough food in winter. Many starve when the snow is deep. But the Key deer can find plenty of nourishing mangrove leaves all year, so they are almost always sleek and healthy.

As weeks go by, the fawns grow quickly. Their mother's milk is very rich. The rainy season comes to the islands. Huge, puffy clouds, like giant cauliflowers, build up in the sky, then turn black. Lightning flashes and rain pours down on the land

and sea. The deer crouch patiently in the shelter of the trees, their coats shedding water. When the rains stop there is drinking water everywhere. The island rocks are as full of holes as a mammoth Swiss cheese, and every hole is brim-full.

The standing water breeds millions of mosquitoes. Sometimes the insects torment the deer, forcing them to go to the shores of the islands. There the ocean breezes blow the mosquitoes away.

During the months that northern people call summer, the fawns begin to eat green plants as well as feeding on their mother's milk. On some days when it is very hot, the doe and her young lie quietly, panting. This is their way of cooling their bodies.

They can also cool off by going into the sea or the shallow island salt marshes. But the salt marshes have mosquitoes and occasional alligators, so the deer do not go there very often.

The sea, with its waves, frightens the fawns while they are still young. As they grow older, they will swim easily from island to island. Adult Key deer churn along briskly, heads well out of the water. When the deer stay on land, they face few natural enemies except the rattlesnake. But once in the sea, they may fall prey to sharks, barracudas, or even crocodiles.

Sometimes a number of does and their fawns will gather together. The first-time mothers usually have only a single fawn. But many of the older does have twins. The bucks are more likely to live alone, or perhaps a father and one or two of his older sons will travel together.

The bucks' antlers grow all through the rainy season. They are covered with "velvet," a tender layer of skin filled with blood vessels that nourish the antlers as they become larger and larger. The older the buck, the more points he is apt to have on his antlers—but he does not always add a new point each year. The youngest bucks have only knobs, or "buttons," where their antlers will later grow. During their second year, they will grow straight, spikelike antlers. The racks, or branched antlers, grow in the following years.

The growing antlers are very sensitive, and the bucks are careful not to bump them.

August, September, and October are the hurricane months. These powerful storms, with winds over 75 miles an hour, are born thousands of miles away in the tropical ocean. Usually they miss the Florida Keys. But when a hurricane does strike, it brings terrible destruction to the islands.

The winds build up huge waves that crash over the low-lying Keys. On the smaller islands, deer may be carried away and drowned. The larger islands have trees blown down or stripped of their leaves. Some of the deer may be injured and some killed; but many survive even the worst hurricane. The fast-growing tropical plants soon clothe the islands in green again, and the deer live as before.

When the rainy season comes to an end, the doe is less and less interested in her fawns. They are old enough now to feed entirely on plants and no longer need her milk. If they try to nurse, she walks away. At first, they may continue to follow her, but soon they go off by themselves.

The fawns cannot understand why they must leave. The doe cannot tell them that the mating season is coming. At that time, usually during the dry season, she will find the buck that will be the father of her young next year.

Northern whitetails almost always mate in the fall. Their young, born in early spring, grow all summer and are large and strong by the time the snow begins to fall. Key deer do not face a cold winter that could kill their newborn young, so their mating time is not as limited as that of northern deer. Key deer may mate or have young at almost any time of year. However, many of them mate in October or November and have young in April or May.

When the bucks' antlers have finished growing, the "velvet" skin becomes dry and the deer rub it against shrubs until it peels off, leaving the antlers hard and sharp. Antlers are weapons, used by the bucks for fighting each other over possession of the does.

With a female deer watching, two rival bucks lower their heads and push at each other with their antlers. Sometimes they inflict wounds with the antlers or their hoofs. More often, the weaker buck simply gives up after a pushing contest and runs away, leaving the winner to mate with the doe.

A strong buck will be able to mate with many does, while a weak buck might not find any mates at all. In this way, it is assured that only the best males will become fathers of the next year's fawns.

There is a mystery about the tiny deer of the Florida Keys. They have not always been dwarfs. Once they were larger, like the whitetail deer that live in the Everglades on the mainland of southern Florida.

How did they become so small?

Sometimes animal bodies change suddenly. A mother may give birth to a baby with a body quite different from her own—perhaps larger, smaller, with a different color, or with some body parts a different shape. This kind of sudden change is called mutation. When the new kind of baby animal grows up, it may have young that look just like it.

There is another kind of change that is much, much slower. It takes hundreds or even thousands of years. Perhaps this was the kind of change that made the deer small. It might have happened like this:

About ten thousand years ago, there were no small deer—and there were no islands, either. At that time, the sea level was much lower than it is now. It was the time of the Ice Age, and much of the earth's water lay on the land in the form of a thick ice cap. All of what is now Florida Bay, including the Keys, was a vast shelf of dry land.

No one knows for certain what this dry land was like. But it surely had whitetail deer living on it—large deer such as those that live on the Florida mainland now.

As hundreds of years went by, the pattern of yearly weather changed. The great ice caps melted. Their water flowed into the sea and the sea slowly became deeper. The lands in Florida Bay were "drowned" by the rising ocean. One long ridge, higher than the rest, still stayed above water. It thrust southwest from the tip of Florida like a finger 150 miles long.

The sea did not rise suddenly. It took hundreds and hundreds of years for the salt waters to cover the Florida Bay lands, and more years for the ridge to become a chain of islands. During this time, several things were making life more difficult for the deer trapped on the islands.

They had more and more difficulty finding food and water. Also, changing weather patterns had turned southern Florida from a cool land with four seasons into a warmer one without any real winter. Large deer cannot stand year-round hot weather as well as smaller ones. Today we find the largest whitetails in northern lands, where their big bodies help them keep warm during cold winters.

Of all the animals, only man can think about his problems and try to solve them by his own efforts. Deer, of course, cannot reason. As human beings, we can think of several ways that the deer might have "solved" the problem of their shrinking, warming homeland:

The deer trapped on the islands could swim back to the Florida mainland, where there was plenty of fresh water and plenty of the food that they were used to.

Or the deer might decrease in numbers as the sea rose. Fewer deer would need less food and water.

But apparently, neither of these things happened. Whitetail deer are not migrating animals. They do not like to travel more than a few miles from their home place. In the North, deer will often starve to death rather than move from a place that has no food into another place several miles away where plant-food is abundant. We can be fairly sure that some large deer living on the islands long ago did become weak from hunger. They did not live as long as they might have if they were well fed. And hot weather also helped make the largest deer sickly and short-lived. No doubt starvation and disease did take a toll of some deer. But then something else began to happen, too.

When the male deer fought during the mating season, the smaller bucks began to win more battles and father more fawns than the larger bucks.

In the cool Northland, the strongest buck is always the largest. But this was not true in the ancient Florida Keys. There, the strongest buck was likely to be the one that needed the least food and water to remain healthy, the one whose body bore up best in the tropical heat. The smaller, stronger bucks won more mating battles and had more offspring than the large, less healthy bucks.

Some of the offspring of the small bucks grew up to be larger than their fathers. In every group of animals, you will always find some that are large and some that are smaller. But it is generally true that small parents have more small young. Also, a doe that does not get all the food she needs is likely to have smaller young.

As hundreds of years went by, the large-sized deer of the Florida Keys became fewer and fewer, while the smaller deer not only increased but also became smaller still. Scientists do not fully understand why the deer decreased in size rather than decreased in numbers, but that seems to be what happened.

The deer changed slowly to fit their changing environment. This kind of change is different from mutation, which happens within a single generation. In adaptation, the babies that grow up, live longest, and have the most young are those whose bodies best fit their environment. Adaptation happens to both plants and animals and it has been going on for as long as life has existed on earth.

By about a thousand years ago, the Key deer had reached the size that they are now, the size that seems to "fit" their island home. Indians lived on the Keys then. But there were not many of them because most of the islands had no permanent fresh water. The Key Indians used some of the tiny deer for food and also ate shellfish and wild plants.

When the first explorers from Europe came to the Keys, about 400 years ago, the islands had large numbers of deer. In later years, Caribbean sailors knew about them and sometimes hunted them for meat.

Black and white settlers began coming to the islands in the early 1800's. Their guns were able to kill deer far more easily than the bows and arrows of the Indians. Men hunted the deer eagerly because there was very little other fresh meat.

The numbers of Key deer diminished quickly as more years passed. They disappeared from all but the largest, wildest

islands. Laws were passed in 1939, forbidding hunting of the deer. But lawbreakers, called poachers, continued to shoot them. By 1949, there were less than 50 of the tiny deer left alive. Most of them lived on the largest island, Big Pine Key.

Thoughtful people loved the tiny deer and wanted to save them. After many years of work by friends of the animals, Congress set up the National Key Deer Refuge in 1957. The illegal hunting was stopped. When the Key deer were no longer hunted, they began to grow numerous again. Today, there are several hundred of them, and their numbers are increasing.

Scientists are studying the Key deer. They hope to learn more about their habits of eating, the way that they reproduce, and the way that they survive in their island environment. They want to compare the adaptation of the tiny deer with the adaptation patterns of other North American whitetail deer.

Visitors can drive to the islands of the tiny deer, traveling the Overseas Highway to the Key Deer Refuge headquarters on Big Pine Key. There are now more than eighteen islands where the Key deer live safely—walking through the forests, swimming in the sea, resting among the tropical plants.

Wildlife of the Florida Keys appearing in this book.